Hip Hop Dance

Marjorie Seevers

xist Publishing

Check out all of the books in the Dancing Through Life Series

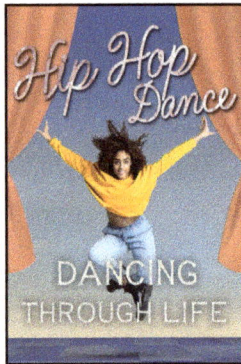

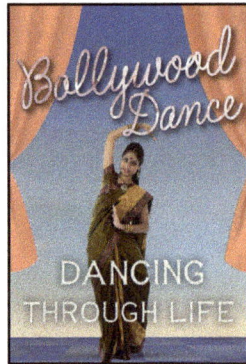

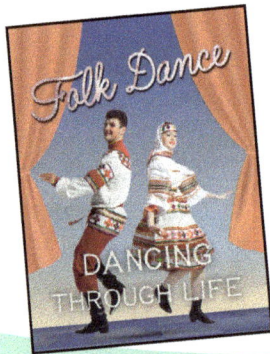

Published in the United States by Xist Publishing
www.xistpublishing.com
© 2025 Copyright Xist Publishing

All images licensed from Adobe Stock

First Edition
Hardcover ISBN: 978-1-5324-5449-3
Paperback ISBN: 978-1-5324-5450-9
eISBN: 978-1-5324-5448-6

PUBLISHED IN TEXAS

Contents

DANCING
THROUGH
LIFE

Chapter 1: What is Hip Hop Dance?

Hip hop dance is a style that started in the streets. It's about being yourself, full of energy, and creative. Unlike other dances, hip hop is loose and free. Dancers make their own moves and follow the beat of the music.

Hip hop dance began in the 1970s in New York City. It was part of a bigger culture with rap music, graffiti art, and DJing. Young people in places like the Bronx started dancing at block parties and on the streets. They wanted to show their skills and have fun with friends. Over time, hip hop dance spread to other cities and countries.

One of the best things about hip hop dance is that there are no strict rules. Dancers can create their own moves and mix styles. Some like to pop and lock, which means moving sharply and quickly. Others like breakdancing, spinning, and flipping on the ground. There are many ways to dance hip hop, and each dancer has their own style.

Hip hop dance is often done in groups called crews. Crews practice together and sometimes compete against other crews in dance battles. These battles are a fun way to show off skills and see who has the best moves.

Hip hop dance is more than just steps and moves. It's a way to be yourself and share your energy with others. Whether you're dancing alone, with friends, or in a crew, hip hop dance is about having fun and being yourself.

The History of Hip Hop Dance: From the Streets to the Stage

Hip hop dance started in the streets of New York City in the 1970s. Young people in the Bronx wanted to create something new and exciting. They began dancing at block parties and in parks. The music was loud, and the energy was high. People showed off their dance moves, and soon hip hop dance was born.

At first, hip hop dance was just for fun. It was a way for people to express themselves and compete with friends. Dancers would gather in a circle, called a cipher. One by one, they stepped into the middle to show their best moves. The cipher became the heart of hip hop dance.

As hip hop dance grew, it spread to other parts of the city and beyond. More and more people wanted to learn these cool new moves. Soon, hip hop dance wasn't just in the streets. It started to appear on TV, in movies, and on stage.

In the 1980s, hip hop dance became even more popular. Dancers formed crews, or groups, to practice and perform together. These crews competed in battles, showing off their skills and creativity. Some of these battles became famous, and people started to see hip hop dance as a real art form.

Over time, hip hop dance moved to big stages and theaters. What started in the streets was now performed for huge audiences. Dancers became stars, and hip hop dance became a part of popular culture around the world.

Today, hip hop dance is taught in schools and studios. It's performed on TV shows, in concerts, and in competitions. What began as a way for young people to have fun and express themselves has grown into a global movement. Hip hop dance is now a powerful way to share stories and creativity with the world.

Chapter 2: Meet the Hip Hop Dancer

Who Can Be a Hip Hop Dancer?

Anyone can be a hip hop dancer! Hip hop dance is for everyone, no matter your age, background, or skill level. It doesn't matter where you come from or how much experience you have. If you love to move and express yourself, you can be a hip hop dancer.

Hip hop dance is about being yourself and having fun. It's a dance style that lets you show your own personality. Some people start dancing when they are young, while others begin later in life. You don't need special training to start. All you need is a love for music and a desire to dance.

Hip hop dancers come in all shapes and sizes. Each dancer brings their own style and energy to the dance. Some dancers are fast and sharp, while others are smooth and flowing. In hip hop, everyone's style is unique, and that's what makes it special. There are many ways to learn hip hop dance. Some people learn by watching videos or joining dance classes. Others practice with friends or join dance crews. No matter how you learn, the most important thing is to keep dancing and having fun.

Hip hop dance is also a great way to stay active and healthy. It's a full-body workout that builds strength, flexibility, and coordination. Plus, dancing to your favorite music is a great way to lift your mood and feel good.

So, who can be a hip hop dancer? The answer is simple: anyone who loves to dance! Whether you're dancing at home, with friends, or in a crew, hip hop dance is for everyone. Just put on some music, start moving, and let your inner dancer shine.

The Different Styles in Hip Hop Dance

Hip hop dance has many different styles. Each style has its own moves, rhythm, and energy. Learning about these styles helps dancers find what they enjoy most.

One popular style is Breaking, also known as breakdancing. This style is full of power and energy. Breakers use their whole body to spin, flip, and move on the ground. Breaking includes moves like windmills, head spins, and freezes, where the dancer holds a pose.

Popping is another hip hop style. Poppers use quick, sharp movements to make their muscles "pop." This style often looks like the dancer is moving like a robot. Popping is fun because it lets dancers play with timing and rhythm.

Locking is a style that is full of fun and surprises. In locking, dancers move quickly and then "lock" into a position, like they are freezing in place. After locking, they quickly move to the next position. Locking is full of personality and often performed with big smiles and high energy.

Another style is Krumping, which is full of emotion and power. Krumping started in the streets as a way to express feelings through dance. Dancers use strong, fast movements. They often dance in battles to show their skills.

Freestyle is a big part of hip hop dance. Freestyle means making up your own moves on the spot. Dancers listen to the music and let their bodies move how they feel. Freestyle is about being creative and expressing yourself.

Each of these styles has its own flavor. Many dancers mix styles to create something new. Hip hop dance is always growing and changing. Dancers are finding new ways to move. No matter which style you choose, hip hop dance is about having fun and being yourself.

Chapter 3: Hip Hop Dance Basics

Basic Steps and Movements

Hip hop dance is full of energy and creativity. It has many basic steps and movements that dancers can use to build their own style. These steps are the building blocks of hip hop dance.

One of the most common moves is the bounce. The bounce is simple but full of energy. Dancers bend their knees and move up and down with the beat. The bounce sets the rhythm for many hip hop dances.

Another basic step is the two-step. In this move, dancers step to the side and bring their feet together. Then, they step to the other side and bring their feet together again. The two-step is easy to learn and can be used with different arm movements to make it more fun.

Body waves are also popular in hip hop dance. To do a body wave, dancers move their body in a smooth, wave-like motion. This move starts at the head and goes down to the feet. Body waves add a cool, flowing look to the dance.

The slide is another basic hip hop move. Dancers slide one foot to the side while dragging the other foot behind. The slide is smooth and adds style to the dance. It can be done quickly or slowly, depending on the music.

Popping and locking are key moves in hip hop. In popping, dancers quickly tighten and relax their muscles to create a "pop." Locking is when dancers freeze in a pose for a moment before moving again. These moves add sharpness and excitement to the dance.

These basic steps and movements are just the beginning. Hip hop dance is all about making these moves your own.

11

Expressing Yourself Through Hip Hop Dance

Hip hop dance is more than just moves. It's a way to express yourself. Through hip hop dance, you can show your feelings, tell a story, and share who you are.

One way to express yourself in hip hop dance is through freestyle. Freestyle means making up your own moves as you go. There are no rules, and you can dance however you feel. The music guides you, and your body moves in a way that feels right. Freestyle lets you be creative and show your unique style.

Facial expressions are also important in hip hop dance. Your face can show how you're feeling while you dance. A smile can show that you're having fun. A serious look can add intensity to your moves. Using your face helps connect your dance with your emotions.

Body language is another way to express yourself. How you move your body can show confidence, excitement, or even sadness. Sharp, quick moves can show power. Slow, smooth moves can show calmness. Your body language tells a story without words. Interacting with others is a big part of hip hop dance. When dancing in a group or with a partner, you can play off each other's energy. You might mirror each other's moves or take turns showing off your skills. This interaction adds fun and connection to the dance.

Music choice also helps you express yourself. The beat, rhythm, and lyrics can inspire different moves and feelings. Fast, upbeat music might make you want to jump and spin. Slow, heavy beats might lead to more grounded and powerful movements. Hip hop dance is all about being yourself. It's a way to let your personality shine. Whether you're dancing alone, with friends, or in front of a crowd, hip hop dance lets you express who you are. Every move, step, and rhythm is a chance to share your story with the world.

Chapter 4: Dressing for Hip Hop Dance

The Hip Hop Dance Outfit: Comfort and Style

When it comes to hip hop dance, what you wear is important. The right outfit helps you move freely and express your style. Hip hop dance outfits are all about comfort and being yourself.

Loose clothing is a key part of hip hop style. Baggy pants, oversized t-shirts, and hoodies are popular choices. These clothes give you the space to move without feeling restricted. Loose clothing also adds a cool, relaxed look to your dance.

Sneakers are the best choice for hip hop dance. They provide support for your feet and allow you to move smoothly. High-tops and low-tops are both popular, depending on your style. Sneakers are not only practical but also a way to show off your personality. Many dancers choose bright colors or unique designs to stand out.

Hats are another common part of the hip hop look. Baseball caps, beanies, or snapbacks add to your style. Hats can be worn forward, backward, or even to the side. They give you a chance to add a personal touch to your outfit.

Accessories like chains, watches, or wristbands are often used in hip hop dance. These items add some flair to your outfit, making your style stand out even more. Just make sure they don't get in the way of your movements.

The hip hop dance outfit is all about comfort and style. It helps you move freely and express who you are. Whether you're dancing on stage, in the studio, or on the streets, your outfit is a big part of your hip hop dance experience. It's not just about looking good—it's about feeling good too.

Accessories and Props in Hip Hop Dance

Accessories and props add extra style to hip hop dance. They help dancers express themselves and stand out. These items are just as important as the moves.
Hats are a favorite in hip hop dance. Baseball caps, beanies, or snapbacks can add to your look. Hats can be worn forward, backward, or to the side. They let dancers add a personal touch to their style.

Chains and jewelry are also common in hip hop. A simple chain around the neck or wrist can add some shine. These items catch the light and make your moves look more exciting. Just make sure your jewelry doesn't get in the way.

Wristbands and watches are often worn too. They add to the overall look and can be useful. A watch can keep you on time, and wristbands can add color to your outfit.

Bandanas are another popular accessory. They can be worn on the head, around the neck, or tied to a wrist. Bandanas add a bold look and show off your personality. Some dancers use props like canes, sticks, or even umbrellas. These props can create interesting moves and add something special to the dance. Props make your performance unique and fun.

Sneakers are both an accessory and a key part of the outfit. Dancers often choose sneakers with bright colors or cool designs. These shoes not only help you dance well but also show off your style.

In hip hop dance, accessories and props are all about making the dance your own. They help you express who you are and make your performance stand out. Whether it's a hat, a chain, or a prop, these items add to the fun and creativity of hip hop dance.

Chapter 5: The Big Performance

Preparing for the Stage

Getting ready for a hip hop performance is exciting. It takes practice and preparation to make sure everything goes well. Dancers need to prepare their bodies, minds, and outfits before stepping onto the stage.

First, dancers practice their moves many times. They learn each step until it feels natural. Practicing helps them feel confident and ready. Dancers often rehearse together as a group. This way, they make sure everyone is moving in sync.

Next, dancers prepare their outfits and accessories. Each piece of clothing should fit well and be comfortable. Dancers try on their outfits to make sure they can move easily. They also check their accessories, like hats or jewelry, to make sure everything is in place.

On the day of the performance, dancers arrive early. They need time to warm up their muscles. Warming up helps prevent injuries and gets their bodies ready to dance. Dancers stretch and do light exercises to prepare.

After warming up, dancers put on their outfits and any makeup. Makeup helps their faces stand out under the stage lights. Dancers might also style their hair to keep it neat during the dance.

Preparing for the stage is a big part of being a dancer. It takes hard work and dedication. But all the effort is worth it when the dancers step into the spotlight and share their hip hop dance with the audience.

The Energy and Fun of Performing Hip Hop Dance

Performing hip hop dance is full of energy and fun. When the music starts, dancers feel the beat, and their bodies move with excitement. The energy from the dance fills the room and spreads to everyone watching.

Hip hop dance is about expressing yourself. On stage, dancers show their personality through their moves. Each dancer brings their own style to the performance. This makes the dance unique and exciting to watch.

The fast beats and strong rhythms of hip hop music pump up the dancers. They jump, spin, and pop with the music, feeling every beat. The crowd's cheers and applause give the dancers even more energy. The connection between the dancers and the audience is strong.

Dancing with others in a group or crew adds to the fun. Dancers move together, showing off their skills. They might take turns stepping forward to do a solo, then come back together for group moves. This teamwork makes the performance exciting.

Hip hop dance performances are lively and unpredictable. Dancers might add freestyle moves or surprise the audience with something new. This keeps the energy high and makes every performance different.

The joy of performing hip hop dance stays with the dancers long after the show. They feel proud and excited to do it again. The energy, creativity, and fun of hip hop dance make every performance special.

Dancing with others in a group or crew adds to the fun. Dancers move together, showing off their skills. They might take turns stepping forward to do a solo, then come back together for group moves. This teamwork makes the performance exciting.

Hip hop dance performances are lively and unpredictable. Dancers might add freestyle moves or surprise the audience with something new. This keeps the energy high and makes every performance different.

The joy of performing hip hop dance stays with the dancers long after the show. They feel proud and excited to do it again. The energy, creativity, and fun of hip hop dance make every performance special.

Conclusion

Hip hop dance is more than just a style of dance. It's a way to express yourself, have fun, and connect with others. From the streets to the stage, hip hop dance brings people together.

Hip hop dance is for everyone. Whether you're new or have danced for years, you can enjoy it. It's a dance where you can show your own style. The moves, the music, and the energy make it special.

As you keep dancing, remember that hip hop is about creativity. Keep practicing, keep learning, and most importantly, keep having fun. Every time you dance, you add to a tradition full of life and energy.

So put on your favorite music, find your groove, and let the rhythm guide you. Hip hop dance is a journey, and every step is a chance to shine. Enjoy the dance, and remember—you are the star of your own show.

Glossary

Body Wave   A flowing movement from head to feet, adding smoothness.

Bounce   A foundational hip hop movement involving bending knees to the beat.

Breaking   Also known as breakdancing, involves dynamic moves like spins and flips.

Cipher   A circle of dancers taking turns performing in the middle.

Crews   Groups of hip hop dancers who practice and compete together.

Freestyle   Improvised, spontaneous dance moves created on the spot..

Krumping   A high-energy dance style expressing intense emotions.

Locking   Quick movements followed by a freeze or "lock" in position.

Popping   A style using sharp muscle movements to create a "pop" effect.

Two-Step   A basic hip hop dance step moving side-to-side.

Stage   The performance area in a theater.

Index

27

www.ingramcontent.com/pod-product-compliance
Lightning Source LLC
LaVergne TN
LVHW070834080426
835508LV00027B/3448